D1243174

GOD'S GRACE

GRACE

for

—

ATHLETES

B&H
PUBLISHING GROUP
NASHVILLE, TENNESSEE

978-1-5359-1720-9

Published by B&H Publishing Group
Nashville, Tennessee

Dewey Decimal Classification: 234.1
Subject Heading: GRACE (THEOLOGY) / HOPE / SELF-CONFIDENCE

1 2 3 4 5 6 7 8 · 22 21 20 19 18

CONTENTS

INTRODUCTION

Life tends to maneuver us into categories, into penciled-in bubbles on the random identification form. Some of them we like; some we don't. Some we actively seek out and continue to pursue; some were sitting there waiting for us and won't turn us loose.

But one thing we all know: deep inside these simple boxes and check marks reside entire worlds crawling with complication, challenge, and difficulty. Even if easy to get into, they are rarely so easy to faithfully, successfully, and steadily keep going through.

As an athlete you may often feel pushed to your limit. You are constantly working to improve your skills, and become better, so that should apply to your Christian walk also . . . right?

The reason this book exists is because God's grace never met a check box it couldn't fill with hope, peace, direction, and perspective—with motivation, counsel, freedom, and opportunity. This book is here, and is now yours, because the Bible not only speaks timelessly to everyone but specifically to you . . . with grace. God's grace. Sufficient to every place. Even to the places you're living this very moment.

ACCEPTANCE

When we are faced with family conflicts, job stresses, uncertainty about the future, or losing the big game we can rest in knowing that God's love for us is constant.

∽

But the LORD said to Samuel, "Do not look at his appearance or his stature because I have rejected him. Humans do not see what the LORD sees, for humans see what is visible, but the LORD sees the heart."
      1 Samuel 16:7

∽

"Everyone the Father gives me will come to me, and the one who comes to me I will never cast out."
      John 6:37

But God proves his own love for us in that while we were still sinners, Christ died for us.
  Romans 5:8

If God is for us, who is against us?
  Romans 8:31

Peter began to speak: "Now I truly understand that God doesn't show favoritism, but in every nation the person who fears him and does what is right is acceptable to him."
  Acts 10:34–35

Heavenly Father, thank You that no matter what trials and stressors I might face, You uphold me and guide me according to Your purposes.

ANGER

Anger is an emotion that can reveal to us our values. The key, however, is not to act out in anger but to speak and act with love.

❧

Refrain from anger and give up your rage;
do not be agitated—it can only bring harm.
        Psalm 37:8

❧

A patient person shows great understanding,
but a quick-tempered one promotes foolishness.
        Proverbs 14:29

❧

A gentle answer turns away anger,
but a harsh word stirs up wrath.
        Proverbs 15:1

"But I tell you, everyone who is angry with his brother or sister will be subject to judgment. Whoever insults his brother or sister, will be subject to the court. Whoever says, 'You fool!' will be subject to hellfire."
    Matthew 5:22

⚬∽

Be angry and do not sin. Don't let the sun go down on your anger, and don't give the devil an opportunity.
    Ephesians 4:26–27

⚬∽

Lord, may Your Holy Spirit guide my words and actions when I'm feeling angry so that I can show grace to my teammates and good sportsmanship behavior to my rivals.

ANXIETY

Beneath our anxieties is a need to feel in control—but our peace is found in knowing that the Creator of the universe holds us safely in the palm of His hand.

"Therefore I tell you: Don't worry about your life, what you will eat or what you will drink; or about your body, what you will wear. Isn't life more than food and the body more than clothing? Consider the birds of the sky: They don't sow or reap or gather into barns, yet your heavenly Father feeds them. Aren't you worth more than they? Can any of you add one moment to his life-span by worrying?"
    Matthew 6:25–27

"Peace I leave with you. My peace I give to you. I do not give to you as the world gives. Don't let your heart be troubled or fearful."
    John 14:27

Don't worry about anything, but in everything, through prayer and petition with thanksgiving, present your requests to God. And the peace of God, which surpasses all understanding, will guard your hearts and minds in Christ Jesus.
Philippians 4:6–7

For God has not given us a spirit of fear, but one of power, love, and sound judgment.
2 Timothy 1:7

Humble yourselves, therefore, under the mighty hand of God, so that he may exalt you at the proper time, casting all your cares on him, because he cares about you.
1 Peter 5:6–7

Heavenly Father, I entrust to You my body, abilities, and actions, knowing that Your peace will guard my heart and mind.

AUTHORITY

As an athlete, you have many different levels of authority surrounding you. You may have a coaching staff, a captain, your family; and to all of them you have the opportunity to reveal to them the very character of God.

For this reason God highly exalted him and gave him the name that is above every name, so that at the name of Jesus every knee will bow—in heaven and on earth and under the earth—and every tongue will confess that Jesus Christ is Lord, to the glory of God the Father.
    Philippians 2:9–11

Jesus came near and said to them, "All authority has been given to me in heaven and on earth."
    Matthew 28:18

Then he said to them, "Give, then, to Caesar the things that are Caesar's, and to God the things that are God's." When they heard this, they were amazed. So they left him and went away.
    Matthew 22:21–22

∽

Let everyone submit to the governing authorities, since there is no authority except from God, and the authorities that exist are instituted by God.
    Romans 13:1

∽

Submit to every human authority because of the Lord, whether to the emperor as the supreme authority or to governors as those sent out by him to punish those who do what is evil and to praise those who do what is good. For it is God's will that you silence the ignorance of foolish people by doing good.
    1 Peter 2:13–15

∽

Father God, please grant me wisdom and grace to be a mirror of godly authority in my life to all those around me, and I willingly submit to Your authority in all situations.

CHANGE

Many changes take place throughout your life, some exciting, some frightening, but God will be with you through them all.

∾

There is an occasion for everything, and a time for every activity under heaven.
    Ecclesiastes 3:1

∾

"Do not remember the past events, pay no attention to things of old. Look, I am about to do something new; even now it is coming. Do you not see it? Indeed, I will make a way in the wilderness, rivers in the desert."
    Isaiah 43:18–19

"Because I, the LORD, have not changed, you descendants of Jacob have not been destroyed."
      Malachi 3:6

Therefore, if anyone is in Christ, he is a new creation; the old has passed away, and see, the new has come!
      2 Corinthians 5:17

Jesus Christ is the same yesterday, today, and forever.
      Hebrews 13:8

Lord Jesus, no matter what the future brings, may I take heart that You are with me until the end of the age.

COMPASSION

The Lord commands us to love our neighbors as ourselves and to love our enemies—godly compassion is speaking and acting out of love in the best interests of others.

Yet he was compassionate;
he atoned for their iniquity
and did not destroy them.
He often turned his anger aside
and did not unleash all of his wrath.
    Psalm 78:38

When he went ashore, he saw a large crowd and had compassion on
them, because they were like sheep without a shepherd. Then he began
to teach them many things.
    Mark 6:34

Carry one another's burdens; in this way you will fulfill the law of Christ.
   Galatians 6:2

And be kind and compassionate to one another, forgiving one another, just as God also forgave you in Christ.
   Ephesians 4:32

Lord, may Your Holy Spirit fill my heart and soul with concern for my family, neighbors, and teammates so that I may be a willing conduit of Your love.

CONFIDENCE

Because we can have full confidence in God, we know that anything we do in His name will come to fruition.

Do not fear, for I am with you;
do not be afraid, for I am your God.
I will strengthen you; I will help you;
I will hold on to you with my righteous right hand.
      Isaiah 41:10

It is not that we are competent in ourselves to claim anything as coming from ourselves, but our adequacy is from God.
      2 Corinthians 3:5

I am able to do all things through him who strengthens me.
      Philippians 4:13

So don't throw away your confidence, which has a great reward. For you need endurance, so that after you have done God's will, you may receive what was promised.

Hebrews 10:35–36

This is how we will know that we belong to the truth and will reassure our hearts before him whenever our hearts condemn us; for God is greater than our hearts, and he knows all things. Dear friends, if our hearts don't condemn us, we have confidence before God and receive whatever we ask from him because we keep his commands and do what is pleasing in his sight.

1 John 3:19–22

Heavenly Father, thank You for Your ultimate faithfulness. I have full confidence that everything that happens is ultimately for the good of those who follow You.

CONFLICT

One way we can walk in the Spirit, rather than according to the flesh, is to resist the pride and need to be right that we often feel in conflicts with others. Remember what is important when competing, and be willing to stand down rather than causing conflict.

Therefore, putting away lying, speak the truth, each one to his neighbor, because we are members of one another. Be angry and do not sin. Don't let the sun go down on your anger, and don't give the devil an opportunity.
    Ephesians 4:25–27

"If your brother sins against you, go and rebuke him in private. If he listens to you, you have won your brother. But if he won't listen, take one or two others with you, so that by the testimony of two or three witnesses every fact may be established. If he doesn't pay attention to them, tell the church. If he doesn't pay attention even to the church, let him be like a Gentile and a tax collector to you."
    Matthew 18:15–17

A gentle answer turns away anger,
but a harsh word stirs up wrath.
    Proverbs 15:1

Bless those who persecute you; bless and do not curse. Rejoice with
those who rejoice; weep with those who weep. Live in harmony with one
another. Do not be proud; instead, associate with the humble. Do not
be wise in your own estimation. Do not repay anyone evil for evil. Give
careful thought to do what is honorable in everyone's eyes. If possible, as
far as it depends on you, live at peace with everyone.
    Romans 12:14–18

What is the source of wars and fights among you? Don't they come from
your passions that wage war within you? You desire and do not have.
You murder and covet and cannot obtain. You fight and wage war. You
do not have because you do not ask.
    James 4:1–2

Lord Jesus, may I imitate Your grace and
gentleness in any disagreement or
confrontation with other people in my life.

CONTENTMENT

The quickest route to contentment is through gratitude and trust—recognize the abundant goodness in your life and trust that God never fails to provide for your needs.

∽

"So don't worry, saying, 'What will we eat?' or 'What will we drink?' or 'What will we wear?' For the Gentiles eagerly seek all these things, and your heavenly Father knows that you need them. But seek first the kingdom of God and his righteousness, and all these things will be provided for you. Therefore don't worry about tomorrow, because tomorrow will worry about itself. Each day has enough trouble of its own."
    Matthew 6:31–34

∽

He then told them, "Watch out and be on guard against all greed, because one's life is not in the abundance of his possessions."
    Luke 12:15

I don't say this out of need, for I have learned to be content in whatever circumstances I find myself. I know both how to make do with little, and I know how to make do with a lot. In any and all circumstances I have learned the secret of being content—whether well fed or hungry, whether in abundance or in need.
Philippians 4:11–12

But godliness with contentment is great gain. For we brought nothing into the world, and we can take nothing out. If we have food and clothing, we will be content with these.
1 Timothy 6:6–8

Keep your life free from the love of money. Be satisfied with what you have, for he himself has said, I will never leave you or abandon you.
Hebrews 13:5

Heavenly Father, thank You for Your unfailing love and faithfulness and may You grow in me a godly contentment.

COURAGE

Having courage doesn't mean that you feel no fear; rather it means having a willingness and readiness to proceed despite the fear.

"Haven't I commanded you: be strong and courageous? Do not be afraid or discouraged, for the LORD your God is with you wherever you go."
Joshua 1:9

I always let the LORD guide me.
Because he is at my right hand,
I will not be shaken.
Psalm 16:8

Wait for the LORD;
be strong, and let your heart be courageous.
Wait for the LORD.
  Psalm 27:14

Be alert, stand firm in the faith, be courageous, be strong.
  1 Corinthians 16:13

For God has not given us a spirit of fear, but one of power, love, and sound judgment.
  2 Timothy 1:7

Dear God, grant me a sense of Your strength and presence that I may face this day and its challenges with courage.

DECEPTION

On any given day, we may be tempted to deceive others—blatant lies, omission of truth, subtle falsehoods—but we are called to have integrity.

The one who lives with integrity lives securely,
but whoever perverts his ways will be found out.
    Proverbs 10:9

Lying lips are detestable to the LORD,
but faithful people are his delight.
    Proverbs 12:22

"You are of your father the devil, and you want to carry out your father's desires. He was a murderer from the beginning and does not stand in the truth, because there is no truth in him. When he tells a lie, he speaks from his own nature, because he is a liar and the father of lies."
   John 8:44

Dear friends, do not believe every spirit, but test the spirits to see if they are from God, because many false prophets have gone out into the world.
   1 John 4:1

Dear God, may Your Spirit empower me to be truthful and loving in all of my encounters.

DEPRESSION

When your heart is heavy and your mind is burdened, hold fast to the truth that God comforts us in all of our afflictions so that we may be able to comfort others with His love.

⁓

The LORD sits enthroned over the flood;
the LORD sits enthroned, King forever.
The LORD gives his people strength;
the LORD blesses his people with peace.
        Psalm 29:10–11

⁓

The LORD is near the brokenhearted;
he saves those crushed in spirit.
        Psalm 34:18

Answer me quickly, LORD;
my spirit fails.
Don't hide your face from me,
or I will be like those
going down to the Pit.
Let me experience
your faithful love in the morning,
for I trust in you.
Reveal to me the way I should go
because I appeal to you.
Psalm 143:7–8

∾

"Do not fear, for I am with you;
do not be afraid, for I am your God.
I will strengthen you; I will help you;
I will hold on to you with my righteous right hand."
Isaiah 41:10

∾

Dear Jesus, You were a man of sorrows
and acquainted with grief—please fill my
heart with Your strength and peace.

DISCIPLINE

Being an athlete means having the self-discipline to improve your skills and strength.

Whoever loves discipline loves knowledge,
but one who hates correction is stupid.
        Proverbs 12:1

The one who will not use the rod hates his son,
but the one who loves him disciplines him diligently.
        Proverbs 13:24

Foolishness is bound to the heart of a youth;
a rod of discipline will separate it from him.
        Proverbs 22:15

Instead, I discipline my body and bring it under strict control, so that after preaching to others, I myself will not be disqualified.
1 Corinthians 9:27

❧

No discipline seems enjoyable at the time, but painful. Later on, however, it yields the peaceful fruit of righteousness to those who have been trained by it.
Hebrews 12:11

❧

Heavenly Father, may Your hand guide me and correct me so that all I do and say will glorify You.

DISCOURAGEMENT

When our hopes are dashed or we fail in an endeavor, we can remember that the God of hope will fill us with joy, peace, and strength.

The LORD is the one who will go before you. He will be with you; he will not leave you or abandon you. Do not be afraid or discouraged.
  Deuteronomy 31:8

"I have told you these things so that in me you may have peace. You will have suffering in this world. Be courageous! I have conquered the world."
  John 16:33

Now may the God of hope fill you with all joy and peace as you believe so that you may overflow with hope by the power of the Holy Spirit.
  Romans 15:13

In the same way the Spirit also helps us in our weakness, because we do not know what to pray for as we should, but the Spirit himself intercedes for us with unspoken groanings. And he who searches our hearts knows the mind of the Spirit, because he intercedes for the saints according to the will of God. We know that all things work together for the good of those who love God, who are called according to his purpose.
    Romans 8:26–28

But he said to me, "My grace is sufficient for you, for my power is perfected in weakness." Therefore, I will most gladly boast all the more about my weaknesses, so that Christ's power may reside in me.
    2 Corinthians 12:9

Lord, sometimes it's hard to remember that You're in control of all things—please grant me Your grace and strength in this moment of discouragement.

DISSATISFIED

When we feel dissatisfied with our lives or how we performed in our most recent game, we can rediscover the abundance around us by practicing gratitude and thanksgiving.

∽

For he has satisfied the thirsty
and filled the hungry with good things.
   Psalm 107:9

∽

The LORD will always lead you, satisfy you in a parched land, and
strengthen your bones. You will be like a watered garden and like a
spring whose water never runs dry.
   Isaiah 58:11

You open your hand
and satisfy the desire of every living thing.
        Psalm 145:16

"I am the bread of life," Jesus told them. "No one who comes to me
will ever be hungry, and no one who believes in me will ever be thirsty
again."
        John 6:35

Now may the God of hope fill you with all joy and peace as you believe
so that you may overflow with hope by the power of the Holy Spirit.
        Romans 15:13

Dear God, no good thing do You withhold from
Your people. Help me see the goodness all around
me and to delight in Your good and perfect gifts.

DRUNKENNESS

No matter what your reasoning, take care to make choices that are godly, healthy, and present a positive witness for the gospel.

For the grace of God has appeared, bringing salvation for all people, instructing us to deny godlessness and worldly lusts and to live in a sensible, righteous, and godly way in the present age, while we wait for the blessed hope, the appearing of the glory of our great God and Savior, Jesus Christ.
    Titus 2:11–13

"Be on your guard, so that your minds are not dulled from carousing, drunkenness, and worries of life, or that day will come on you unexpectedly like a trap. For it will come on all who live on the face of the whole earth. But be alert at all times, praying that you may have strength to escape all these things that are going to take place and to stand before the Son of Man."
    Luke 21:34–38

Wine is a mocker, beer is a brawler;
whoever goes astray because of them is not wise.
     Proverbs 20:1

Let us walk with decency, as in the daytime: not in carousing and
drunkenness; not in sexual impurity and promiscuity; not in quarreling
and jealousy.
     Romans 13:13

So don't be foolish, but understand what the Lord's will is. And don't get
drunk with wine, which leads to reckless living, but be filled by the Spirit:
speaking to one another in psalms, hymns, and spiritual songs, singing
and making music with your heart to the Lord, giving thanks always
for everything to God the Father in the name of our Lord Jesus Christ,
submitting to one another in the fear of Christ.
     Ephesians 5:17–21

Lord God, may my heart and soul overflow with
the joy of knowing You, and let this joy be my
strength in moments of weakness. Help me to walk in
Your ways, and pursue the life that You want for me.

ENCOURAGEMENT

We can experience deep gladness from knowing that our God goes before us and is with us at all times.

The LORD is the one who will go before you. He will be with you; he will not leave you or abandon you. Do not be afraid or discouraged.
   Deuteronomy 31:8

God is our refuge and strength,
a helper who is always found in times of trouble.
   Psalm 46:1

"Aren't five sparrows sold for two pennies? Yet not one of them is forgotten in God's sight. Indeed, the hairs of your head are all counted. Don't be afraid; you are worth more than many sparrows."
   Luke 12:6–7

"I have told you these things so that in me you may have peace. You will have suffering in this world. Be courageous! I have conquered the world."
  John 16:33

And let us watch out for one another to provoke love and good works, not neglecting to gather together, as some are in the habit of doing, but encouraging each other, and all the more as you see the day approaching.
  Hebrews 10:24–25

Christ Jesus, may Your Spirit strengthen and encourage my heart today so that I may be a source of encouragement for those I encounter throughout the day.

EXCESS

Stress and uncertainty can lead us to eating too much, working long hours away from the family, or hoarding our resources, but believers are called to trust in God's sufficiency.

He answered, "It is written: Man must not live on bread alone but on every word that comes from the mouth of God."
    Matthew 4:4

He then told them, "Watch out and be on guard against all greed, because one's life is not in the abundance of his possessions."
    Luke 12:15

Don't you know that your body is a temple of the Holy Spirit who is in you, whom you have from God? You are not your own, for you were bought at a price. So glorify God with your body.
  1 Corinthians 6:19–20

Do not love the world or the things in the world. If anyone loves the world, the love of the Father is not in him. For everything in the world—the lust of the flesh, the lust of the eyes, and the pride in one's possessions—is not from the Father, but is from the world. And the world with its lust is passing away, but the one who does the will of God remains forever.
  1 John 2:15–17

Dear God, help me trust in You more deeply so I find in You everything I need.

FAILURE

Though failures of any kind can crush our spirits, we have the assurance that God's purposes can never be thwarted.

A person's steps are established by the LORD,
and he takes pleasure in his way.
Though he falls, he will not be overwhelmed,
because the LORD supports him with his hand.
    Psalm 37:23–24

He brought me up from a desolate pit,
out of the muddy clay,
and set my feet on a rock,
making my steps secure.
He put a new song in my mouth,
a hymn of praise to our God.
Many will see and fear,
and they will trust in the LORD.
    Psalm 40:2–3

And not only that, but we also rejoice in our afflictions, because we know that affliction produces endurance, endurance produces proven character, and proven character produces hope.

Romans 5:3–4

❧

Now we have this treasure in clay jars, so that this extraordinary power may be from God and not from us. We are afflicted in every way but not crushed; we are perplexed but not in despair; we are persecuted but not abandoned; we are struck down but not destroyed.

2 Corinthians 4:7–9

❧

Brothers and sisters, I do not consider myself to have taken hold of it. But one thing I do: Forgetting what is behind and reaching forward to what is ahead, I pursue as my goal the prize promised by God's heavenly call in Christ Jesus.

Philippians 3:13–14

❧

Heavenly Father, grant me grace in times of failure and help me press forward as I fix my eyes on Jesus.

FAITHFULNESS

God's everlasting faithfulness to His people is a deep source of hope, as well as an inspiration for how we should conduct ourselves in our relationships.

Because of the LORD's faithful love
we do not perish,
for his mercies never end.
They are new every morning;
great is your faithfulness!
        Lamentations 3:22–23

"His master said to him, 'Well done, good and faithful servant! You were faithful over a few things; I will put you in charge of many things. Share your master's joy.'"
        Matthew 25:21

"Whoever is faithful in very little is also faithful in much, and whoever is unrighteous in very little is also unrighteous in much. So if you have not been faithful with worldly wealth, who will trust you with what is genuine? And if you have not been faithful with what belongs to someone else, who will give you what is your own?"
Luke 16:10–12

✍

If we are faithless, he remains faithful, for he cannot deny himself.
2 Timothy 2:13

✍

Let us hold on to the confession of our hope without wavering, since he who promised is faithful.
Hebrews 10:23

✍

Dear God, whose mercies are new every morning, grant me wisdom to be faithful to my team, my family, my church, and my community.

FEAR

Most of our dread comes not from an immediate threat but from fear of what might happen—but this is false fear. We have an almighty God who loves us and cares for us at all times.

"Haven't I commanded you: be strong and courageous? Do not be afraid or discouraged, for the LORD your God is with you wherever you go."
        Joshua 1:9

When I am afraid,
I will trust in you.
        Psalm 56:3

You did not receive a spirit of slavery to fall back into fear. Instead, you received the Spirit of adoption, by whom we cry out, "Abba, Father!"
    Romans 8:15

For God has not given us a spirit of fear, but one of power, love, and sound judgment.
    2 Timothy 1:7

Humble yourselves, therefore, under the mighty hand of God, so that he may exalt you at the proper time, casting all your cares on him, because he cares about you.
    1 Peter 5:6–7

Abba, Father, I cry out to You for Your protection and comfort in times when I'm afraid. Thank You for Your faithful love and comfort.

FORGIVENESS

Forgiving someone who has hurt you means you no longer call to mind their fault or error. This extends grace to them and freedom for you.

⌘

"Therefore I tell you, her many sins have been forgiven; that's why she loved much. But the one who is forgiven little, loves little."
    Luke 7:47

⌘

Live in harmony with one another. Do not be proud; instead, associate with the humble. Do not be wise in your own estimation. Do not repay anyone evil for evil. Give careful thought to do what is honorable in everyone's eyes. If possible, as far as it depends on you, live at peace with everyone.
    Romans 12:16–18

Be kind and compassionate to one another, forgiving one another, just as God also forgave you in Christ.
Ephesians 4:32

❦

As God's chosen ones, holy and dearly loved, put on compassion, kindness, humility, gentleness, and patience, bearing with one another and forgiving one another if anyone has a grievance against another. Just as the Lord has forgiven you, so you are also to forgive.
Colossians 3:12–13

❦

Dear God, just as You forgave all my debts and wrongs through Christ, empower me to extend forgiveness to those who have mistreated or hurt me.

FRIENDSHIP

Precious are the friends, neighbors, and colleagues in our lives who faithfully stand by us through joys and sorrows, victories and failures, gains and loss.

∽

Iron sharpens iron,
and one person sharpens another.
        Proverbs 27:17

∽

Two are better than one because they have a good reward for their efforts. For if either falls, his companion can lift him up; but pity the one who falls without another to lift him up.
        Ecclesiastes 4:9–10

"No one has greater love than this: to lay down his life for his friends. You are my friends if you do what I command you. I do not call you servants anymore, because a servant doesn't know what his master is doing. I have called you friends, because I have made known to you everything I have heard from my Father."
    John 15:13–15

Dear friends, let us love one another, because love is from God, and everyone who loves has been born of God and knows God.
    1 John 4:7

Therefore encourage one another and build each other up as you are already doing.
    1 Thessalonians 5:11

Lord Jesus, who called His disciples friends, thank You for demonstrating God's love for us and how best to love one another.

GRACE

The greatest gift we will ever receive is grace—the wholly unmerited favor of the Most High.

The law came along to multiply the trespass. But where sin multiplied, grace multiplied even more.
    Romans 5:20

For sin will not rule over you, because you are not under the law but under grace.
    Romans 6:14

Now if by grace, then it is not by works; otherwise grace ceases to be grace.
    Romans 11:6

But he said to me, "My grace is sufficient for you, for my power is perfected in weakness." Therefore, I will most gladly boast all the more about my weaknesses, so that Christ's power may reside in me.

    2 Corinthians 12:9

∞

For you are saved by grace through faith, and this is not from yourselves; it is God's gift—not from works, so that no one can boast.

    Ephesians 2:8–9

∞

Lord God, thank You for Your riches of grace that have been poured out on me through faith in Christ Jesus.

GUILT

Guilt does not have to consume us because we know there is no condemnation for those in Christ Jesus.

As far as the east is from the west,
so far has he removed
our transgressions from us.
    Psalm 103:12

"Come, let us settle this,"
says the LORD. "Though your sins are scarlet,
they will be as white as snow;
though they are crimson red,
they will be like wool."
    Isaiah 1:18

Therefore, there is now no condemnation for those in Christ Jesus, because the law of the Spirit of life in Christ Jesus has set you free from the law of sin and death.

Romans 8:1–2

☙

In him we have redemption through his blood, the forgiveness of our trespasses, according to the riches of his grace.

Ephesians 1:7

☙

If we confess our sins, he is faithful and righteous to forgive us our sins and to cleanse us from all unrighteousness.

1 John 1:9

☙

Lord, when I have fallen short, please grant me the wisdom to confess my sins and be cleansed of all unrighteousness.

HAPPINESS

Though happiness sometimes comes from external circumstances, we experience the most lasting happiness by enjoying our union with Christ.

෴

Therefore my heart is glad
and my whole being rejoices;
my body also rests securely.
      Psalm 16:9

෴

Take delight in the LORD,
and he will give you your heart's desires.
      Psalm 37:4

A joyful heart makes a face cheerful,
but a sad heart produces a broken spirit.
        Proverbs 15:13

I know that there is nothing better for them than to rejoice and enjoy the
good life.
        Ecclesiastes 3:12

Rejoice in the Lord always. I will say it again: Rejoice!
        Philippians 4:4

Lord Jesus, may my heart be happy
and cheerful because I know You.

HONOR

Our culture tends to be informal and irreverent, but as believers, we can stand apart by showing honor and respect to everyone we encounter.

Honor the LORD with your possessions
and with the first produce of your entire harvest;
then your barns will be completely filled,
and your vats will overflow with new wine.
        Proverbs 3:9–10

Now to the King eternal, immortal, invisible, the only God, be honor
and glory forever and ever. Amen.
        1 Timothy 1:17

Pray for us, for we are convinced that we have a clear conscience,
wanting to conduct ourselves honorably in everything.
Hebrews 13:18

∽

Honor everyone. Love the brothers and sisters. Fear God. Honor the
emperor.
1 Peter 2:17

∽

Lord God, may Your Spirit guide me to honor You
with my speech, actions, time, and resources today.

HOPE

It's tempting to put our hope in the wrong places—relationships, financial security, personal, or professional abilities—but our firmest hope is found only in Christ Jesus.

But those who trust in the LORD
will renew their strength;
they will soar on wings like eagles;
they will run and not become weary,
they will walk and not faint.
    Isaiah 40:31

We have also obtained access through him by faith into this grace in which we stand, and we rejoice in the hope of the glory of God. And not only that, but we also rejoice in our afflictions, because we know that affliction produces endurance, endurance produces proven character, and proven character produces hope.
    Romans 5:2–4

I wait for the LORD;
I wait and put my hope in his word.
    Psalm 130:5

∽

Now may the God of hope fill you with all joy and peace as you believe
so that you may overflow with hope by the power of the Holy Spirit.
    Romans 15:13

∽

Let us run with endurance the race that lies before us, keeping our eyes
on Jesus, the source and perfecter of our faith. For the joy that lay before
him, he endured the cross, despising the shame, and sat down at the
right hand of the throne of God. For consider him who endured such
hostility from sinners against himself, so that you won't grow weary and
give up.
    Hebrews 12:1–3

∽

Lord of hope, please fill me with all
joy and peace as I hope in You.

HUMILITY

The key to cultivating true humility isn't to be self-deprecating but to simply not think of oneself much at all.

❦

Sitting down, he called the Twelve and said to them, "If anyone wants to be first, he must be last and servant of all."
   Mark 9:35

❦

Live in harmony with one another. Do not be proud; instead, associate with the humble. Do not be wise in your own estimation.
   Romans 12:16

❦

Do nothing out of selfish ambition or conceit, but in humility consider others as more important than yourselves.
   Philippians 2:3

Adopt the same attitude as that of Christ Jesus, who, existing in the form of God, did not consider equality with God as something to be exploited. Instead he emptied himself by assuming the form of a servant, taking on the likeness of humanity. And when he had come as a man, he humbled himself by becoming obedient to the point of death—even to death on a cross.

Philippians 2:5–8

Who among you is wise and understanding? By his good conduct he should show that his works are done in the gentleness that comes from wisdom.

James 3:13

Lord Jesus, who demonstrated perfect selflessness, please be my vision and my constant focus so that I forget myself completely.

IMPULSIVENESS

The feeling that most reliably follows an impulsive word or action is regret.

Discretion will watch over you,
and understanding will guard you.
It will rescue you from the way of evil—
from anyone who says perverse things.
    Proverbs 2:11–12

So if you have been raised with Christ, seek the things above, where Christ is, seated at the right hand of God. Set your minds on things above, not on earthly things.
    Colossians 3:1–2

For we all stumble in many ways. If anyone does not stumble in what he says, he is mature, able also to control the whole body.

    James 3:2

❧

Watch yourselves so you don't lose what we have worked for, but that you may receive a full reward. Anyone who does not remain in Christ's teaching but goes beyond it does not have God. The one who remains in that teaching, this one has both the Father and the Son.

    2 John 8–9

❧

Lord God, I am confident that I will see Your goodness in the land of the living. May Your Spirit empower me to be strong and wait for You.

INTEGRITY

The late basketball coach John Wooden once said, "The true test of a person's character is what he does when no one is watching."

∾

The one who lives with integrity lives securely,
but whoever perverts his ways will be found out.
    Proverbs 10:9

∾

Better the poor person who lives with integrity
than the rich one who distorts right and wrong.
    Proverbs 28:6

∾

Indeed, we are giving careful thought to do what is right, not only before
the Lord but also before people.
    2 Corinthians 8:21

Whatever you do, do it from the heart, as something done for the Lord and not for people, knowing that you will receive the reward of an inheritance from the Lord. You serve the Lord Christ.
   Colossians 3:23–24

❧

Yet do this with gentleness and respect, keeping a clear conscience, so that when you are accused, those who disparage your good conduct in Christ will be put to shame.
   1 Peter 3:16

❧

Search me, Lord God, and know my heart,
and if there is anything ungodly in me,
lead me in the way everlasting.

JOY

Happiness can be fleeting, but joy is steadfast because it comes from the firm foundation of our intimacy with Christ.

ॐ

You reveal the path of life to me;
in your presence is abundant joy;
at your right hand are eternal pleasures.
> *Psalm 16:11*

ॐ

This is the day the LORD has made;
let us rejoice and be glad in it.
> *Psalm 118:24*

But the fruit of the Spirit is love, joy, peace, patience, kindness, goodness, faithfulness, gentleness, and self-control. The law is not against such things.
    Galatians 5:22–23

⟡

"As the Father has loved me, I have also loved you. Remain in my love. If you keep my commands you will remain in my love, just as I have kept my Father's commands and remain in his love. I have told you these things so that my joy may be in you and your joy may be complete."
    John 15:9–11

⟡

Dear Jesus, thank You for the abundant joy that comes from Your faithful presence.

JUSTICE

God's Word makes it clear how deeply He cares about the poor and the oppressed, and He calls us to act accordingly.

Do not act unjustly when deciding a case. Do not be partial to the poor or give preference to the rich; judge your neighbor fairly.
  Leviticus 19:15

Isn't this the fast I choose: To break the chains of wickedness, to untie the ropes of the yoke, to set the oppressed free, and to tear off every yoke? Is it not to share your bread with the hungry, to bring the poor and homeless into your house, to clothe the naked when you see him, and not to ignore your own flesh and blood?
  Isaiah 58:6–7

The LORD of Armies says this: "Make fair decisions. Show faithful love and compassion to one another. Do not oppress the widow or the fatherless, the resident alien or the poor, and do not plot evil in your hearts against one another."
Zechariah 7:9–10

༐

Don't be deceived: God is not mocked. For whatever a person sows he will also reap,
Galatians 6:7

༐

Pure and undefiled religion before God the Father is this: to look after orphans and widows in their distress and to keep oneself unstained from the world.
James 1:27

༐

Father God, please open my eyes and heart to the needs in my community and empower me to bring Your light to dark corners.

KINDNESS

In God's great kindness, He saved us through His beloved Son, and He now calls us to extend that same gentleness and compassion to others.

He also raised us up with him and seated us with him in the heavens in Christ Jesus, so that in the coming ages he might display the immeasurable riches of his grace through his kindness to us in Christ Jesus.
    Ephesians 2:6–7

Let all bitterness, anger and wrath, shouting and slander be removed from you, along with all malice. And be kind and compassionate to one another, forgiving one another, just as God also forgave you in Christ.
    Ephesians 4:31–32

Therefore, as God's chosen ones, holy and dearly loved, put on compassion, kindness, humility, gentleness, and patience.
    Colossians 3:12

But when the kindness of God our Savior and his love for mankind appeared, he saved us—not by works of righteousness that we had done, but according to his mercy—through the washing of regeneration and renewal by the Holy Spirit.
    Titus 3:4–5

Dear God, may Your Holy Spirit soften my speech and actions so that I display Your kindness to everyone I encounter today.

KNOWLEDGE

Though you gain knowledge in many different ways, including experience, the truest knowledge is having awe and reverence for the Creator.

∾

For wisdom will enter your heart,
and knowledge will delight you.
    Proverbs 2:10

∾

The mind of the discerning acquires knowledge,
and the ear of the wise seeks it.
    Proverbs 18:15

∾

For the earth will be filled with the knowledge of the LORD's glory, as the water covers the sea.
    Habakkuk 2:14

We know that "we all have knowledge." Knowledge puffs up, but love builds up. If anyone thinks he knows anything, he does not yet know it as he ought to know it. But if anyone loves God, he is known by him.

1 Corinthians 8:1–3

For this reason also, since the day we heard this, we haven't stopped praying for you. We are asking that you may be filled with the knowledge of his will in all wisdom and spiritual understanding, so that you may walk worthy of the Lord, fully pleasing to him: bearing fruit in every good work and growing in the knowledge of God, being strengthened with all power, according to his glorious might, so that you may have great endurance and patience, joyfully giving thanks to the Father, who has enabled you to share in the saints' inheritance in the light.

Colossians 1:9–12

*Lord, may Your Spirit teach me Your Word
and guide me in Your perfect ways.*

LAZINESS

Whether laundry and household chores, practicing in the field, or pushing through to the final buzzer, work of all kinds is a gift from God to provide us with opportunities to learn and grow and to serve others.

∽

The slacker craves, yet has nothing,
but the diligent is fully satisfied.
          Proverbs 13:4

∽

The one who is lazy in his work
is brother to a vandal.
          Proverbs 18:9

Whatever you do, do it from the heart, as something done for the Lord and not for people, knowing that you will receive the reward of an inheritance from the Lord. You serve the Lord Christ.
  Colossians 3:23–24

In fact, when we were with you, this is what we commanded you: "If anyone isn't willing to work, he should not eat."
  2 Thessalonians 3:10

Lord, when I'm feeling tired and unmotivated, please strengthen me with the power of Your Holy Spirit.

LEADERSHIP

A true leader isn't one who has climbed to the top of a hierarchy, but one who chooses to be a servant above all else. Even if you do not have an official role of leadership, you can still be a leader to those around you.

Jesus called them over and said, "You know that the rulers of the Gentiles lord it over them, and those in high positions act as tyrants over them. It must not be like that among you. On the contrary, whoever wants to become great among you must be your servant, and whoever wants to be first among you must be your slave; just as the Son of Man did not come to be served, but to serve, and to give his life as a ransom for many."

Matthew 20:25–28

Shepherd God's flock among you, not overseeing out of compulsion but willingly, as God would have you; not out of greed for money but eagerly; not lording it over those entrusted to you, but being examples to the flock. And when the chief Shepherd appears, you will receive the unfading crown of glory.

1 Peter 5:2–4

Adopt the same attitude as that of Christ Jesus, who, existing in the form of God, did not consider equality with God as something to be exploited. Instead he emptied himself by assuming the form of a servant, taking on the likeness of humanity. And when he had come as a man, he humbled himself by becoming obedient to the point of death—even to death on a cross. For this reason God highly exalted him and gave him the name that is above every name, so that at the name of Jesus every knee will bow—in heaven and on earth and under the earth—and every tongue will confess that Jesus Christ is Lord, to the glory of God the Father.

    Philippians 2:5–11

Don't let anyone despise your youth, but set an example for the believers in speech, in conduct, in love, in faith, and in purity.

    1 Timothy 4:12

*Lord Jesus, You came not to be served
but to serve—please grant me Your Spirit
of servant leadership in my endeavors.*

LONELINESS

Modern life has left many of us feeling isolated—but thanks to God's faithful presence and our community of believers, we never have to be alone.

❧

"My presence will go with you, and I will give you rest."
    Exodus 33:14

❧

The LORD is the one who will go before you. He will be with you; he will not leave you or abandon you. Do not be afraid or discouraged.
    Deuteronomy 31:8

❧

God provides homes for those who are deserted.
He leads out the prisoners to prosperity,
but the rebellious live in a scorched land.
    Psalm 68:6

He heals the brokenhearted
and bandages their wounds.
    Psalm 147:3

✑

Blessed be the God and Father of our Lord Jesus Christ, the Father of mercies and the God of all comfort. He comforts us in all our affliction, so that we may be able to comfort those who are in any kind of affliction, through the comfort we ourselves receive from God.
    2 Corinthians 1:3–4

✑

Father of mercies, please comfort me in times of loneliness so that I may be a comfort to others.

MERCY

When the demands of life overwhelm you, remember that you can approach God's throne of grace with boldness.

❧

"Blessed are the merciful, for they will be shown mercy."
    Matthew 5:7

❧

"Go and learn what this means: I desire mercy and not sacrifice. For I didn't come to call the righteous, but sinners."
    Matthew 9:13

❧

Therefore, let us approach the throne of grace with boldness, so that we may receive mercy and find grace to help us in time of need.
    Hebrews 4:16

Speak and act as those who are to be judged by the law of freedom. For judgment is without mercy to the one who has not shown mercy. Mercy triumphs over judgment.

James 2:12–13

Blessed be the God and Father of our Lord Jesus Christ. Because of his great mercy he has given us new birth into a living hope through the resurrection of Jesus Christ from the dead.

1 Peter 1:3

Lord God, thank You for Your mercy and lovingkindness in times of need.

MOTIVES

Rather than self-seeking or people-pleasing, we should endeavor to do all things through genuine love for God and others. This becomes difficult when it comes to competing. Never let yourself become absorbed by the need to win.

∽

But the LORD said to Samuel, "Do not look at his appearance or his stature because I have rejected him. Humans do not see what the LORD sees, for humans see what is visible, but the LORD sees the heart."
   1 Samuel 16:7

∽

All a person's ways seem right to him,
but the LORD weighs hearts.
   Proverbs 21:2

For am I now trying to persuade people, or God? Or am I striving to please people? If I were still trying to please people, I would not be a servant of Christ.
Galatians 1:10

❧

Do nothing out of selfish ambition or conceit, but in humility consider others as more important than yourselves.
Philippians 2:3

❧

Instead, just as we have been approved by God to be entrusted with the gospel, so we speak, not to please people, but rather God, who examines our hearts.
1 Thessalonians 2:4

❧

Lord, please weigh my heart and my reasons for doing the things I do, and reveal to me any motives that don't glorify You.

OBEDIENCE

Obedience to God means yielding our will to His, and His will is that we love Him and our neighbor as ourselves. We can model a heart of obedience (not perfection) and one that desires to honor God in all we do.

∽

I have chosen the way of truth;
I have set your ordinances before me.
    Psalm 119:30

∽

"If you love me, you will keep my commands."
    John 14:15

∽

Peter and the apostles replied, "We must obey God rather than people."
    Acts 5:29

The one who keeps his commands remains in him, and he in him. And the way we know that he remains in us is from the Spirit he has given us.
    1 John 3:24

ᔐ

For this is what love for God is: to keep his commands. And his commands are not a burden, because everyone who has been born of God conquers the world. This is the victory that has conquered the world: our faith.
    1 John 5:3–4

ᔐ

Lord Jesus, may Your Spirit guide me in all my thoughts, words, and actions that I may be fully submitted to Your will.

PATIENCE

The adrenaline rushing in sports can rattle your nerves, but take care to avoid making wrong choices or damaging your relationships.

✑

The end of a matter is better than its beginning; a patient spirit is better than a proud spirit.
   Ecclesiastes 7:8

✑

Now if we hope for what we do not see, we eagerly wait for it with patience.
   Romans 8:25

✑

My dear brothers and sisters, understand this: Everyone should be quick to listen, slow to speak, and slow to anger, for human anger does not accomplish God's righteousness.
   James 1:19–20

Therefore, brothers and sisters, be patient until the Lord's coming. See how the farmer waits for the precious fruit of the earth and is patient with it until it receives the early and the late rains. You also must be patient. Strengthen your hearts, because the Lord's coming is near.
   James 5:7–8

The Lord does not delay his promise, as some understand delay, but is patient with you, not wanting any to perish but all to come to repentance.
   2 Peter 3:9

Heavenly Father, You are patient and slow to anger—please help me be still and wait patiently for You.

PEACE

Rather than worry over what has happened in the past or what might happen in the future, be still with the Lord in the peace of the present moment.

∽

You will keep the mind that is dependent on you in perfect peace, for it is trusting in you.
    Isaiah 26:3

∽

"Peace I leave with you. My peace I give to you. I do not give to you as the world gives. Don't let your heart be troubled or fearful."
    John 14:27

For I am persuaded that neither death nor life, nor angels nor rulers, nor things present nor things to come, nor powers, nor height nor depth, nor any other created thing will be able to separate us from the love of God that is in Christ Jesus our Lord.
    Romans 8:38–39

And the peace of God, which surpasses all understanding, will guard your hearts and minds in Christ Jesus. Finally brothers and sisters, whatever is true, whatever is honorable, whatever is just, whatever is pure, whatever is lovely, whatever is commendable—if there is any moral excellence and if there is anything praiseworthy—dwell on these things.
    Philippians 4:7–8

*Lord Jesus, may Your perfect peace guard
my heart and mind as I trust in You.*

PERSEVERANCE

No matter what trial you face or how exhausted you may feel, remember that the Lord holds you and strengthens you at all times.

And not only that, but we also rejoice in our afflictions, because we know that affliction produces endurance, endurance produces proven character, and proven character produces hope. This hope will not disappoint us, because God's love has been poured out in our hearts through the Holy Spirit who was given to us.
        Romans 5:3–5

Therefore, since we also have such a large cloud of witnesses surrounding us, let us lay aside every hindrance and the sin that so easily ensnares us. Let us run with endurance the race that lies before us, keeping our eyes on Jesus, the source and perfecter of our faith. For the joy that lay before him, he endured the cross, despising the shame, and sat down at the right hand of the throne of God.
        Hebrews 12:1–2

Let us not get tired of doing good, for we will reap at the proper time if we don't give up.
    Galatians 6:9

Consider it a great joy, my brothers and sisters, whenever you experience various trials, because you know that the testing of your faith produces endurance. And let endurance have its full effect, so that you may be mature and complete, lacking nothing.
    James 1:2–4

Blessed is the one who endures trials, because when he has stood the test he will receive the crown of life that God has promised to those who love him.
    James 1:12

Dear Jesus, help me fix my eyes on You that Your Spirit may strengthen my heart and will to persevere.

POWER

An athlete's greatest power lies in his or her ability to submit to the wisdom and guidance of the Holy Spirit within.

❧

"But you will receive power when the Holy Spirit has come on you, and you will be my witnesses in Jerusalem, in all Judea and Samaria, and to the end of the earth."
    Acts 1:8

❧

For the kingdom of God is not a matter of talk but of power.
    1 Corinthians 4:20

But he said to me, "My grace is sufficient for you, for my power is perfected in weakness." Therefore, I will most gladly boast all the more about my weaknesses, so that Christ's power may reside in me.
   2 Corinthians 12:9

⌘

For God has not given us a spirit of fear, but one of power, love, and sound judgment.
   2 Timothy 1:7

⌘

*Dear Jesus, when I feel weak or powerless,
I look to You for Your grace and strength.*

PRAISE

There are many ways to praise the Lord God beyond singing songs in church—when you live from a place of love and gratitude, your entire life becomes an act of praise and worship.

*I will praise God's name with song
and exalt him with thanksgiving.*
    Psalm 69:30

*Hallelujah!
Praise God in his sanctuary.
Praise him in his mighty expanse.
Praise him for his powerful acts;
praise him for his abundant greatness.*
    Psalm 150:1–2

For from him and through him and to him are all things. To him be the glory forever. Amen.
       Romans 11:36

Now to him who is able to protect you from stumbling and to make you stand in the presence of his glory, without blemish and with great joy, to the only God our Savior, through Jesus Christ our Lord, be glory, majesty, power, and authority before all time, now and forever. Amen.
       Jude 24–25

Lord Jesus, from You and through You and to You are all things—to You be the glory forever and ever, amen!

PRAYER

No matter how we come to the Lord, whether to present our requests or to sit silently in His presence, we can trust that He hears us.

"Whenever you pray, you must not be like the hypocrites, because they love to pray standing in the synagogues and on the street corners to be seen by people. Truly I tell you, they have their reward. But when you pray, go into your private room, shut your door, and pray to your Father who is in secret. And your Father who sees in secret will reward you. When you pray, don't babble like the Gentiles, since they imagine they'll be heard for their many words. Don't be like them, because your Father knows the things you need before you ask him.

"Therefore, you should pray like this: Our Father in heaven, your name be honored as holy. Your kingdom come. Your will be done on earth as it is in heaven. Give us today our daily bread. And forgive us our debts, as we also have forgiven our debtors. And do not bring us into temptation, but deliver us from the evil one.

"For if you forgive others their offenses, your heavenly Father will forgive you as well. But if you don't forgive others, your Father will not forgive your offenses."

Matthew 6:5–15

"If you remain in me and my words remain in you, ask whatever you want and it will be done for you."
  John 15:7

In the same way the Spirit also helps us in our weakness, because we do not know what to pray for as we should, but the Spirit himself intercedes for us with unspoken groanings.
  Romans 8:26

Don't worry about anything, but in everything, through prayer and petition with thanksgiving, present your requests to God.
  Philippians 4:6

Pray constantly.
  1 Thessalonians 5:17

Lord Jesus, just as You taught your followers how to pray, instill in me a deep desire to seek Your presence.

PRIDE

Though we may be blessed with wisdom and success, we can avoid arrogance by remembering that our position in leadership is service to God.

∽

When arrogance comes, disgrace follows,
but with humility comes wisdom.
    Proverbs 11:2

∽

Everyone with a proud heart is detestable to the LORD;
be assured, he will not go unpunished.
    Proverbs 16:5

A person's pride will humble him,
but a humble spirit will gain honor.
        Proverbs 29:23

Live in harmony with one another. Do not be proud; instead, associate
with the humble. Do not be wise in your own estimation.
        Romans 12:16

For if anyone considers himself to be something when he is nothing, he
deceives himself.
        Galatians 6:3

Father God, please forgive the ways I puff myself up
rather than humble myself under Your loving hand.

PURITY

Keeping yourself pure goes beyond refraining from sexual behavior—it's living a life that is free from the corruptible aspects of worldly culture so that your body, mind, and soul are centered on God.

❧

God, create a clean heart for me
and renew a steadfast spirit within me.
    Psalm 51:10

❧

"Blessed are the pure in heart, for they will see God."
    Matthew 5:8

❧

But put on the Lord Jesus Christ, and don't make plans to gratify the
desires of the flesh.
    Romans 13:14

Flee sexual immorality! Every other sin a person commits is outside the body, but the person who is sexually immoral sins against his own body.
    1 Corinthians 6:18

∽

If we confess our sins, he is faithful and righteous to forgive us our sins and to cleanse us from all unrighteousness.
    1 John 1:9

∽

Dear God, please create a clean heart for me and renew a steadfast spirit within me, so that I may live in purity before You.

PURPOSE

Our deepest purpose is not in what we do but in who we are—people who love, honor, and praise God.

When all has been heard, the conclusion of the matter is this: fear God and keep his commands, because this is for all humanity.
        Ecclesiastes 12:13

"My Father is glorified by this: that you produce much fruit and prove to be my disciples."
        John 15:8

But I consider my life of no value to myself; my purpose is to finish my course and the ministry I received from the Lord Jesus, to testify to the gospel of God's grace.
        Acts 20:24

He has saved us and called us with a holy calling, not according to our works, but according to his own purpose and grace, which was given to us in Christ Jesus before time began.

　　　2 Timothy 1:9

Sing to him; sing praise to him; tell about all his wondrous works! Honor his holy name; let the hearts of those who seek the Lord rejoice.

　　　1 Chronicles 16:9–10

Lord Jesus, may each day offer me
opportunities to live out my truest purpose
by loving and serving You and those around me.

RELATIONSHIPS

Loving relationships and friendships are gifts from God—we are built up and supported in community and in fellowship with other believers.

∽

Then the LORD God said, "It is not good for the man to be alone. I will make a helper corresponding to him."
    Genesis 2:18

∽

But if they do not have self-control, they should marry, since it is better to marry than to burn with desire.
    1 Corinthians 7:9

Don't become partners with those who do not believe. For what partnership is there between righteousness and lawlessness? Or what fellowship does light have with darkness?
2 Corinthians 6:14

Therefore encourage one another and build each other up as you are already doing.
1 Thessalonians 5:11

Above all, maintain constant love for one another, since love covers a multitude of sins.
1 Peter 4:8

Heavenly Father, reveal to me ways I can be a conduit of Your love toward those in my community today.

RELIABILITY

In modern society, some people think little of "flaking" on others, but believers can stand apart by being dependable and committed to our word. This especially comes into play when it comes to being reliable for your teammates.

He will not allow your foot to slip;
your Protector will not slumber.
    Psalm 121:3

"But let your 'yes' mean 'yes,' and your 'no' mean 'no.' Anything more
than this is from the evil one."
    Matthew 5:37

Whoever is faithful in very little is also faithful in much, and whoever is unrighteous in very little is also unrighteous in much.
    Luke 16:10

What you have heard from me in the presence of many witnesses, commit to faithful men who will be able to teach others also.
    2 Timothy 2:2

Lord, just as You are constant and faithful, help me to be a leader that my people can reliably depend upon.

SACRIFICE

Our willingness to sacrifice our money, possessions, time, energy, and attention attests to our faith in God's abundant provision in all things. What are you holding back from God?

"This is my command: Love one another as I have loved you. No one has greater love than this: to lay down his life for his friends. You are my friends if you do what I command you."
    John 15:12–14

But God proves his own love for us in that while we were still sinners, Christ died for us.
    Romans 5:8

Don't neglect to do what is good and to share, for God is pleased with such sacrifices.
    Hebrews 13:16

When they arrived at the place that God had told him about, Abraham built the altar there and arranged the wood. He bound his son Isaac and placed him on the altar on top of the wood. Then Abraham reached out and took the knife to slaughter his son. But the angel of the Lord called to him from heaven and said, "Abraham, Abraham!" He replied, "Here I am."

Then he said, "Do not lay a hand on the boy or do anything to him. For now I know that you fear God, since you have not withheld your only son from me." Abraham looked up and saw a ram caught in the thicket by its horns. So Abraham went and took the ram and offered it as a burnt offering in place of his son. And Abraham named that place The Lord Will Provide, so today it is said: "It will be provided on the Lord's mountain."

Then the angel of the Lord called to Abraham a second time from heaven and said, "By myself I have sworn," this is the Lord's declaration: "Because you have done this thing and have not withheld your only son, I will indeed bless you and make your offspring as numerous as the stars of the sky and the sand on the seashore. Your offspring will possess the city gates of their enemies. And all the nations of the earth will be blessed by your offspring because you have obeyed my command."

Genesis 22:9–18

Father God, just as You did not withhold your own Son, grant me a heart willing to give of my gifts and blessings for the good of others.

SAVIOR

Christ Jesus is our Savior, the Source and Perfecter of our faith, who for the joy set before Him endured the cross.

He said, "They are indeed my people, children who will not be disloyal," and he became their Savior. In all their suffering, he suffered, and the angel of his presence saved them. He redeemed them because of his love and compassion; he lifted them up and carried them all the days of the past.
    Isaiah 63:8–9

My soul praises the greatness of the Lord, and my spirit rejoices in God my Savior, because he has looked with favor on the humble condition of his servant.
    Luke 1:46–48

"This Jesus is the stone rejected by you builders, which has become the cornerstone. There is salvation in no one else, for there is no other name under heaven given to people by which we must be saved."
    Acts 4:11–12

❧

This is good, and it pleases God our Savior, who wants everyone to be saved and to come to the knowledge of the truth.
    1 Timothy 2:3–4

❧

And we have seen and we testify that the Father has sent his Son as the world's Savior.
    1 John 4:14

❧

*Lord Jesus, I have been crucified with You—
may the life I now live be lived for You who
loved me and gave Yourself for me.*

SELF-CONTROL

We often think about self-control in terms of moral behavior, but consider also the importance of refraining from angry speech—especially when reacting on social media.

A person who does not control his temper
is like a city whose wall is broken down.
    Proverbs 25:28

No temptation has come upon you except what is common to humanity.
But God is faithful; he will not allow you to be tempted beyond what you
are able, but with the temptation he will also provide a way out so that
you may be able to bear it.
    1 Corinthians 10:13

Finally brothers and sisters, whatever is true, whatever is honorable, whatever is just, whatever is pure, whatever is lovely, whatever is commendable—if there is any moral excellence and if there is anything praiseworthy—dwell on these things.
Philippians 4:8

Be sober-minded, be alert. Your adversary the devil is prowling around like a roaring lion, looking for anyone he can devour.
1 Peter 5:8

Lord God, when I struggle with temptation or am quick to anger, please renew Your gentle Spirit within me.

SERVICE

Christ Jesus, the King of heaven, came not to be served but to serve others and set for us His example to follow.

And the King will answer them, "Truly I tell you, whatever you did for one of the least of these brothers and sisters of mine, you did for me."
   Matthew 25:40

For even the Son of Man did not come to be served, but to serve, and to give his life as a ransom for many.
   Mark 10:45

I have been crucified with Christ, and I no longer live, but Christ lives in me. The life I now live in the body, I live by faith in the Son of God, who loved me and gave himself for me.

   Galatians 2:20

Therefore, my dear brothers and sisters, be steadfast, immovable, always excelling in the Lord's work, because you know that your labor in the Lord is not in vain.

   1 Corinthians 15:58

Lord Jesus, please open my eyes to see the myriad of opportunities to serve my teammates, family, coach, church, and community, and open my heart to do so freely and with compassion.

SPEECH

When we speak, the words we choose are only part of our response—we must also consider our motives and tone of voice.

❧

A gentle answer turns away anger,
but a harsh word stirs up wrath.
> *Proverbs 15:1*

❧

Let your speech always be gracious, seasoned with salt, so that you may know how you should answer each person.
> *Colossians 4:6*

❧

Bless those who persecute you; bless and do not curse.
> *Romans 12:14*

But no one can tame the tongue. It is a restless evil, full of deadly poison. With the tongue we bless our Lord and Father, and with it we curse people who are made in God's likeness. Blessing and cursing come out of the same mouth. My brothers and sisters, these things should not be this way.

   James 3:8–10

No foul language should come from your mouth, but only what is good for building up someone in need, so that it gives grace to those who hear.
   Ephesians 4:29

Holy Spirit, please fill my heart with the gracious love of God so that my speech is humble, gentle, and kind.

STRENGTH

Our greatest source of strength is trusting in the power and love of God, who provides grace in our times of weakness.

❧

My flesh and my heart may fail,
but God is the strength of my heart,
my portion forever.
    Psalm 73:26

❧

If I say, "My foot is slipping,"
your faithful love will support me, LORD.
    Psalm 94:18

But he said to me, "My grace is sufficient for you, for my power is perfected in weakness." Therefore, I will most gladly boast all the more about my weaknesses, so that Christ's power may reside in me. So I take pleasure in weaknesses, insults, hardships, persecutions, and in difficulties, for the sake of Christ. For when I am weak, then I am strong.
    2 Corinthians 12:9–10

Consider it a great joy, my brothers and sisters, whenever you experience various trials, because you know that the testing of your faith produces endurance.
    James 1:2–3

Lord Jesus, Your grace is sufficient for me—may Your power be perfected in my moments of weakness.

STRESS

Chronic stress is quickly becoming a national crisis that threatens our health and well-being—but God has reassured us that He is our ever-present helper in times of trouble.

❧

Cast your burden on the LORD,
and he will sustain you;
he will never allow the righteous to be shaken.
      Psalm 55:22

❧

Commit your activities to the LORD,
and your plans will be established.
      Proverbs 16:3

For I am the LORD your God, who holds your right hand, who says to you, "Do not fear, I will help you."
   Isaiah 41:13

"Come to me, all of you who are weary and burdened, and I will give you rest. Take up my yoke and learn from me, because I am lowly and humble in heart, and you will find rest for your souls. For my yoke is easy and my burden is light."
   Matthew 11:28–30

I am able to do all things through him who strengthens me.
   Philippians 4:13

Dear God, please strengthen me by Your Spirit when I feel overwhelmed, exhausted, and uncertain.

SUCCESS

Whether you succeed or fail at leading your group or organization, your true identity is your relationship with the Lord Jesus.

∽

Take delight in the LORD,
and he will give you your heart's desires.
Psalm 37:4

∽

Commit your activities to the LORD,
and your plans will be established.
Proverbs 16:3

"For what will it benefit someone if he gains the whole world yet loses his life? Or what will anyone give in exchange for his life? For the Son of Man is going to come with his angels in the glory of his Father, and then he will reward each according to what he has done."
Matthew 16:26–27

Humble yourselves before the Lord, and he will exalt you.
James 4:10

Lord Jesus, no matter how well I lead my people or succeed in our goals, help me remember that my purpose is to be a shining beacon of Your light and love.

TEMPTATION

No temptation that you may face is ever unavoidable—
God is faithful to provide an escape from what tempts
you.

*"Stay awake and pray, so that you won't enter into temptation. The
spirit is willing, but the flesh is weak."*
   Matthew 26:41

*No temptation has come upon you except what is common to humanity.
But God is faithful; he will not allow you to be tempted beyond what you
are able, but with the temptation he will also provide a way out so that
you may be able to bear it.*
   1 Corinthians 10:13

For since he himself has suffered when he was tempted, he is able to help those who are tempted.
    Hebrews 2:18

∾

No one undergoing a trial should say, "I am being tempted by God," since God is not tempted by evil, and he himself doesn't tempt anyone. But each person is tempted when he is drawn away and enticed by his own evil desire. Then after desire has conceived, it gives birth to sin, and when sin is fully grown, it gives birth to death.
    James 1:13–15

∾

Therefore, submit to God. Resist the devil, and he will flee from you.
    James 4:7

∾

Lord God, my spirit is willing, but my flesh is weak—please help me to honor You in all of my choices.

THANKFULNESS

The more we practice gratitude and thanksgiving, the more abundance and goodness we recognize all around us.

⌀

Give thanks to the LORD, for he is good;
his faithful love endures forever.
        Psalm 118:1

⌀

For we know that the one who raised the Lord Jesus will also raise us with Jesus and present us with you. Indeed, everything is for your benefit so that, as grace extends through more and more people, it may cause thanksgiving to increase to the glory of God.
        2 Corinthians 4:14–16

Let the word of Christ dwell richly among you, in all wisdom teaching and admonishing one another through psalms, hymns, and spiritual songs, singing to God with gratitude in your hearts.
    Colossians 3:16

Rejoice always, pray constantly, give thanks in everything; for this is God's will for you in Christ Jesus.
    1 Thessalonians 5:16–18

Every good and perfect gift is from above, coming down from the Father of lights, who does not change like shifting shadows.
    James 1:17

Father of lights, I praise You and thank You for every good and perfect gift You have given.

TRUST

To trust the Lord is to believe what He has said about Himself: He is good, faithful, and sovereign.

The person who trusts in the Lord, whose confidence indeed is the Lord, is blessed. He will be like a tree planted by water: it sends its roots out toward a stream, it doesn't fear when heat comes, and its foliage remains green. It will not worry in a year of drought or cease producing fruit.
    Jeremiah 17:7–8

Wait for the LORD;
be strong, and let your heart be courageous.
Wait for the LORD.
    Psalm 27:14

I will be with you when you pass through the waters, and when you pass through the rivers, they will not overwhelm you. You will not be scorched when you walk through the fire, and the flame will not burn you.
    Isaiah 43:2

And my God will supply all your needs according to his riches in glory in Christ Jesus.
    Philippians 4:19

This is the confidence we have before him: If we ask anything according to his will, he hears us.
    1 John 5:14

Dear God, thank You that all things work together for the good of those who love You and are called according to Your purpose.

VICTORY

We can take joy knowing that it is not up to us to fight all of our battles, but to rest in the strength and sufficiency of God. True victory comes not from our own strength on the field, but from trust in God.

For the LORD your God is the one who goes with you to fight for you against your enemies to give you victory.
    Deuteronomy 20:4

Though a righteous person falls seven times,
he will get up,
but the wicked will stumble into ruin.
    Proverbs 24:16

"I have told you these things so that in me you may have peace. You will have suffering in this world. Be courageous! I have conquered the world."

John 16:33

The sting of death is sin, and the power of sin is the law. But thanks be to God, who gives us the victory through our Lord Jesus Christ!

1 Corinthians 15:56–57

Then I heard a loud voice from the throne: Look, God's dwelling is with humanity, and he will live with them. They will be his peoples, and God himself will be with them and will be their God. He will wipe away every tear from their eyes. Death will be no more; grief, crying, and pain will be no more, because the previous things have passed away.

Revelation 21:3–4

Christ Jesus, it is through You that all of my victories are won—please strengthen me today with a sense of Your presence.

VIOLENCE

Whether brute force or abusive language, Jesus stood against all forms of violence and oppression, submitting even to death on a cross.

❧

The LORD examines the righteous,
but he hates the wicked
and those who love violence.
Psalm 11:5

❧

Don't envy a violent man
or choose any of his ways.
Proverbs 3:31

"You have heard that it was said, An eye for an eye and a tooth for a tooth. But I tell you, don't resist an evildoer. On the contrary, if anyone slaps you on your right cheek, turn the other to him also."
Matthew 5:38–39

Then Jesus told him, "Put your sword back in its place because all who take up the sword will perish by the sword. Or do you think that I cannot call on my Father, and he will provide me here and now with more than twelve legions of angels?"
Matthew 26:52–53

Heavenly Father, help me realize that all the violence in the world originates in our human hearts, even mine. Cleanse us and make us people of peace.

WISDOM

Though we may have knowledge and years of experience, true wisdom comes from the Holy Spirit, who helps us discern what is true, good, and right.

◈

Teach us to number our days carefully
so that we may develop wisdom in our hearts.
    Psalm 90:12

◈

Do not be conformed to this age, but be transformed by the renewing
of your mind, so that you may discern what is the good, pleasing, and
perfect will of God.
    Romans 12:2

Yet to those who are called, both Jews and Greeks, Christ is the power of God and the wisdom of God, because God's foolishness is wiser than human wisdom, and God's weakness is stronger than human strength.
    1 Corinthians 1:24–25

※

Now if any of you lacks wisdom, he should ask God—who gives to all generously and ungrudgingly—and it will be given to him.
    James 1:5

※

Heavenly Father, who gives generously and freely, please fill me with Your wisdom for how to live a life that is pleasing to You.

WORK

Our ability to work is a gift from God—we can create, serve, and produce for the good of the world around us, which glorifies the Creator.

❧

*Commit your activities to the Lord,
and your plans will be established.*
Proverbs 16:3

❧

Do everything in love.
1 Corinthians 16:14

❧

And God is able to make every grace overflow to you, so that in every way, always having everything you need, you may excel in every good work.
2 Corinthians 9:8

Whatever you do, do it from the heart, as something done for the Lord and not for people, knowing that you will receive the reward of an inheritance from the Lord. You serve the Lord Christ.

Colossians 3:23–24

Come now, you who say, "Today or tomorrow we will travel to such and such a city and spend a year there and do business and make a profit." Yet you do not know what tomorrow will bring—what your life will be! For you are like vapor that appears for a little while, then vanishes. Instead, you should say, "If the Lord wills, we will live and do this or that."

James 4:13–15

Creator of all good things, grant me meaningful work and empower me to do everything for You and not for people.

VERSE INDEX